92223

SIXTY-ONE PSALMS OF DAVID

David R. Slavitt, ed. & trans. Oxford. 18.95 **3.98**

This book is not so much another translation as
an inspired and engagingly fresh rendition of the
Psalms. Following the tradition of Ezra Pound's
versions and Robert Lowell's *Imitations*, David
R. Slavitt—himself an esteemed poet and transla-
tor of Ovid, Virgil, Seneca, and others—casts the
Psalms into a modern idiom that stays faithful to
the original but strikes the ear remarkably like
contemporary speech. Here the Psalms are com-
pressed, clarified, and given the satisfying shapes
and textures of English poetry. Working most
often in rhymed tetrameter quatrains, but also
employing rhymed couplets and other forms,
Slavitt brings all the subtlety and expressive
power of English versification to these Psalms,
and the result is a poetry that fits comfortably in
the lineage that includes Sir Philip Sidney, John
Donne, William Blake, and Richard Wilbur.
"In Slavitt's hands the Psalms become an intense,
one-sided conversation with God. They cohere as
only a fine book of poems can, unified by the
poet's voice. The full range of emotions emerges,
especially fear, disgust at the foibles of humanity,
loathing of one's enemies, and awe and trust in
God."—Howard Schwartz   (150/96)

PHONE:
1-800-395-2665
OR 410-309-2705

FAX:
1-800-866-5578
OR 410-309-2707

91974
SEASONED TIMBER
Dorothy Canfield Fisher.
New England (pap) 16.95 **3.98**
Originally published in 1939, Dorothy Canfield
Fisher's last novel is remarkably prescient in its
defense of human rights and the ramifications of
their denial. "Nobody values anything for its
endurance nowadays," muses T.C.Hulme, head-
master of the Clifford Vermont Academy. Long
devoted to the school and to his eccentric aunt,
T.C. is increasingly aware that life is passing him
by. A brief stab at late-love collapses, and then a
rich, out-of-state trustee dies and leaves the
Academy a million-dollar "gift" in his will.
However, there are strings—Jews must be exclud-
ed, girls ousted, and local students squeezed out
by a tuition hike. In *Seasoned Timber,* Fisher, who
was named by Eleanor Roosevelt as one of the ten
most influential women in the United States,
addresses socio-economic class divisions, racism,
gender bias, and educational funding. Yet her
work is more than a blazing form of journalism. If
intellectual substance, depth of feeling, and narra-
tive skill are any indication, Fisher's final novel
was certainly written with her whole personality.
"Incredibly rich in character and ideas, folk stuff
and everyday life, rugged Vermonters and dry
humor, realistic romance and muted tragedy."
—*LATimes* (489/96)

Sixty-One Psalms of David

David R. Slavitt

Sixty-One Psalms of David

NEW YORK   OXFORD

Oxford University Press

1996

OXFORD UNIVERSITY PRESS

Oxford New York Athens Auckland Bangkok Calcutta
Cape Town Dar es Salaam Delhi Florence Hong Kong Istanbul
Karachi Kuala Lumpur Madras Madrid Melbourne Mexico City
Nairobi Paris Singapore Taipei Tokyo Toronto
and associated companies in
Berlin Ibadan

Library of Congress Cataloging-in-Publication Data

Bible. O.T. Psalms. English. Slavitt. Selections. 1996.
    Sixty-One Psalms of David / [translated by] David R. Slavitt.
       p. cm.
     ISBN 0-19-510711-X
     I. Slavitt, David R., 1935–   . II. Title.
  BS1424.S52   1996
  223´ .205209—dc20   96-8719

1 3 5 7 9 8 6 4 2

Printed in the United States of America
on acid-free paper

FOR BARBARA

AND IN MEMORY OF JASON

Preface

THE PSALMS are wonderfully passionate poems in which faith and doubt dance together in the clarity of desert sunshine. The emotional strength of this collection of hymns, complaints, dirges, and celebrations is immediately engaging. Both for artistic and spiritual reasons, men and women have turned to this book of the Bible more frequently than to any other.

The pieces here are not so much translations — excellent and scrupulous translations of the Bible are widely available — as they are renditions. Or perhaps one might call them meditations on the originals. I have tried to see through the text to the gestures that enliven the poems. The tradition of the psalms begins with King David's pretending to the simplicity of a shepherd, which is a gesture not very much different from what Virgil later contrived in his pastoral representations of sophisticated Romans in the *Eclogues*. And over the centuries, other psalmists worked their variations of David's voice both in homage to the originator of the form and to gain the rhetorical advantage that convention affords. Much of the power of the psalms comes, I suspect, from their faux naif quality and its suggestion of the unqualified kind of belief in a personal God many of us had when we were children. As adults we may or may not still believe in that way, but most of us feel at the least a nostalgia, a sense of loss of that confidence in a sometimes strict but always loving deity.

My attempt here is to suggest by means of the instrumentalities of English poetry and, indeed, nursery poetry, that child-like directness with which the psalmist addresses his God. Purists may object that the Hebrew doesn't rhyme in this way. (Neither does Homer rhyme, except in Pope's version.) There is, nevertheless, a delight in purely linguistic display. Several of the psalms — and I have reproduced a couple of them — are acrostics, skittering their way through the order of the Hebrew alphabet in a manner that is perhaps playful, perhaps a virtuoso performance, but also an

indication that this kind of speech is not normal, but arti-
factual. The feat is one that claims a degree of heightened
awareness if not actual inspiration.

My rhymes and games are intended in that same spirit,
and for the sake of that same directness of spirituality. The
enterprise itself is hardly unprecedented. Thomas Wyatt's
Seven Penitential Psalms were published posthumously in 1549.
And there was a complete collection of the "Sydnean"
Psalms, by Sir Philip Sidney (who did the first 43) and his
sister, Mary, the Countess of Pembroke who finished the
work after his death. These poems were not published but
were circulated in manuscript and John Donne admired
them, writing, in "Upon the translation of the Psalmes by
Sir Philip Sydney, and the Countess of Pembroke his Sister"

> Though some have, some may some Psalmes translate,
> We thy Sydnean Psalmes shall celebrate,
> And, till we come th'Extemporall song to sing,
> (Learned the first hower [hour], that we see the King,

Who has translated those translators) may
These their sweet learned labours, all the way
Be as our tuning, that, when hence we part
We may fall in with them, and sing our part.

There were later poets who did complete versions of the Psalms, notably George Wither (1632), George Sandys (1636), Isaac Watts (1719) and Christopher Smart (1765), and a number of poets did a few here and there — as a very young man, Milton did a couple of adaptations of the psalms, perhaps as exercises, which he liked well enough to preserve. Henry Vaughan did a small number of similar Englishings.

The enterprise has not been much attempted in recent times. And yet these are poems of such power and vividness that they invite our attention, offering themselves as subjects for the modern American idiom. I was curious to see what it would do to them and them to it. I wanted them, in Donne's fine phrase, to "be as our tuning."

My intention here is in no way to supplant the more scholarly and scrupulous renditions into English. I have not even thought of doing the entire set of 150, but have tried to speak for those pieces — roughly a third of them — that spoke to me. Some of the psalms are repetitive, alternate versions of the same poem; some are fragments or mere introductions; and some, perhaps because of defects in the manuscripts, have omissions that make their sense, at the very best, obscure. There are even various systems for numbering the psalms. (I follow the Revised Standard Version.) Sixty-one seemed a good number, all the more attractive to me because it happens to be my age.

This collection is a series of efforts to recreate wherever I could what I take to be the powerful emotional charge of the originals by whatever linguistic strategies I could find. If, after glancing at these re-enactments, the reader then were to turn to a more scrupulous version — that of the Jewish Publication Society, or of the Revised Standard Version, or of the King James Version — or even perhaps to the original Hebrew, I should be heartily pleased both as a poet and a teacher. There are also scholarly studies of the psalms, most notably those of Moses Buttenweiser and, more recently, Hans-Joachim Kraus which serious students may wish to consult.

To be, at the same time, poet and teacher is the heart of the art of translation. These are not altogether consonant roles, but their tension makes the enterprise all the more challenging and rewarding.

Contents

THE PSALMS

	Psalm 1	*3*
	Psalm 3	*4*
	Psalm 5	*6*
	Psalm 6	*10*
	Psalm 10	*12*
	Psalm 11	*14*
	Psalm 12	*16*
	Psalm 15	*17*
	Psalm 17	*18*
	Psalm 19	*21*
	Psalm 22	*23*
	Psalm 23	*27*
	Psalm 24	*29*
	Psalm 25	*31*
	Psalm 29	*33*

Psalm 34	34
Psalm 39	36
Psalm 41	38
Psalm 47	40
Psalm 49	41
Psalm 51	43
Psalm 52	45
Psalm 53	47
Psalm 55	49
Psalm 56	52
Psalm 58	54
Psalm 59	56
Psalm 63	59
Psalm 67	61
Psalm 69	62

Psalm 70	66
Psalm 71	67
Psalm 77	70
Psalm 79	72
Psalm 82	74
Psalm 83	76
Psalm 87	79
Psalm 88	80
Psalm 93	82
Psalm 97	83
Psalm 100	85
Psalm 102	86
Psalm 103	89
Psalm 109	92
Psalm 113	96

Psalm 114   97

Psalm 115   98

Psalm 120   100

Psalm 121   101

Psalm 124   102

Psalm 126   104

Psalm 127   106

Psalm 130   107

Psalm 131   109

Psalm 133   110

Psalm 136   111

Psalm 137   114

Psalm 139   116

Psalm 144   118

Psalm 150   120

Sixty-One Psalms of David

I

Happy is he who does not harken
to wickedness, nor stand with the sinner,
nor sit with the scoffer, nor let such darken
his delight in the Lord's law,
for he has learned to bask in the inner
light of the word. He thrives like a tree
that has grown up by some riverbank.
Verdant, its leafy branches draw
those birds whose twitterings praise and thank
the giver of all our gifts below
beneficent heaven. It is not so
with the wicked who, if they also fly,
are like the chaff that the winds blow
in the great threshing of judgment. I
shall delight to watch as they are cast out
from the camp of the righteous, each and all,
for the Lord marks — as who can doubt? —
and wickedness at the last must fall.

3

Lord, how many enemies
I have! How many fists they raise
against me! How many calumnies
I bear! They say that I am beyond
all help, even Yours. I turn my gaze
upward, hopeless, foolish, fond . . .
                              I do. Tra la la la.

And You will be a shield to keep
me safe, a helmet for my head —
or a crown of glory. When I weep
You'll harken to my spirit's bother
just as a father or a mother
does, and I shall be comforted.
                              I will. Tra la la la.

And in these hard and hostile places,
I shall lie down and sleep sound
although ten thousand brutish faces
menace me from all around,
for should they come too close, You'll smite
those who do wickedness in Your sight.
                              You will. Tra la la la.

Smash them and break their teeth, oh break
their tiniest bones — not for Your servant,
too needy, insufficiently fervent,
but rather Your own glory's sake.
Deliverance is the Lord's alone.
Your blessings be upon Your own
                              who'll sing, tra la la la.

5

I groan all night.
O Lord, give ear
to the words I voice
in my sad plight.
I quake with fear
but then rejoice
in the morning light
when hope renews
and I recite
loud and clear
the prayers of the Jews.

Do You delight
in wickedness
or evil? No,
the boastful may

not stand before
Your glaring eyes.
Neither can they
who utter lies,
for You abhor
bloodthirstiness
and falsehood. You
will ruin them
for what they do.

I enter in
at Your temple door
or face it from
wherever I am
and worship for
deliverance. Oh,

lead me, good Lord,
along the straight
path of Your words
I have learned to love.
Help me to win
against my foe
and endure the hate
of the speakers of
foul slanders. All
their hearts are false.
Their mouths are great
abysmal holes
like rifled tombs.
When Your judgment comes,
condemn their souls
and let them fall

under the weight
of their grievous faults.

But those who believe
in the Lord, let them
in gladness sing
as they receive
Your favors. Bring
blessings upon
Jerusalem.

6

In righteous anger, Lord, do not
chastise me, but be gracious to
a man in torment. What I've got
is pain that goes from the bone right through
to the soul. You are my only cure.
How long, O Lord, can I endure?

Deliver me, dear Lord, and save
my life not for my sake but Yours.
There is only silence in the grave:
no chorus of praise and gratitude pours
from the house of the dead. All night I weep
in woe and longing, never sleep,

but toss and turn while my tears soak
my pillow sodden. My eyes are red . . .
But my complaint may yet provoke
the Lord's attention, so those who'd shed
my blood may learn to fear His name
and turn away their heads in shame.

10

O Lord, why do You keep your distance
when we are so severely tried?
While the poor and weak pray for assistance
and the wicked prey on them, You hide.
The rich are ravenous and grow
fat, while the poor still suffer so.
Can You not let both parties know
that You are the Lord? The greedy preen,
renounce their heavenly king and say
there is no God. Cruel and serene
in their unbelief, they live the lie
their mouths have uttered. Like lions they
batten upon the weak who cry
aloud to an impassive heaven
that God forgets them and hides His face.
For their despair, may they be forgiven.
Such suffering calls out for grace.
Arise, then, Lord; lift up Your hand

against the wicked to chastise
their arrogance; make them understand
what justice is; and under Your skies
let there be no place for them to hide.
With comfort, meanwhile, Lord, come to
those who invoke Your holy name,
but also to the wicked who
defy You, visiting pain and shame
upon them. Break their bones, and fill
their fouled hearts with Your cleansing purges.
Those you cannot purify, kill,
and let us who have suffered watch
as our tormentors suffer the scourges
You surely have prepared for such
as dare disturb Your kingdom's peace,
until their wickedness shall cease,
and the poor at last have our release.

II

In the Lord alone, do I
take refuge; therefore do not say
that like a sparrow I should fly
to hide in the mountains far away.
Don't speak of how they bend the bow,
fit their arrows onto the strings,
and shoot to bring the upright low.
Do not complain that, these days, things
are ruined, rotten, out of whack,
and righteousness cannot come back . . .

for the Lord is in His holy temple.
His throne in heaven does not shake.
His gaze is steady, clear, and simple.
His tests of men make no mistake.
He judges good and wickedness,

and His soul hates the souls that hate.
On every sinner, He shall wait
with burning coals of sulfurous flame
and searing winds, but the good He'll bless.
Decent men who love His name
shall be rewarded and lifted high
and see His countenance by and by.

12

Help us, O God: there are no good
people left who behave as they should.
Everyone lies, deceives, and flatters.
Slice off their lips and cut to tatters
those sinuous tongues they exercise for
defrauding the helpless, weak, and poor.
Our groans of suffering must impress
the Lord who will surely come to bless
and save His beleaguered people who trust
His promises. His words are just
and sure as silver that's purified
for the seventh time. On every side
the wicked prowl; the vile exult.
Protect us, O God! Punish their guilt.

15

O Lord, who may enter into Your
tent or dwell upon Your hill?
He who walks blamelessly before
You, does what is right, and never will
speak slander with his tongue or do
wrong to his neighbor; he'll despise
the wicked, but honor those who are true
to the Lord; he will not realize
profits from someone else's distress
or prey upon innocent helplessness.
A man like that cannot be moved:
a rock, he is warmed in the Lord's love.

17

Hear my just complaint, O Lord.
Give ear to my cry. The prayer of my mouth
is not deceitful. To my word
attend and let vindication come,
as your keen eye discerns the truth.
Try my heart! Surprise me at some

unexpected moment to see
if I be false. In the tasks of men
and by Your laws, I have kept free
of violence or any other taint,
treading only Your paths. Now when
I turn to You with my complaint,

the wonders of Your love, display.
Protector of the wronged and weak,

hold my enemies at bay.
Keep me the apple of Your eye;
enfold me in Your wing. They seek
to do me harm. Lord, hear my cry!

They close their hearts to pity; they
defy, insult with curling lip;
they track me down. I am their prey.
Like lions, they slaver, ready to tear
my flesh when I am in their grip.
Help me, Lord! Arise, I say!

Deliver my life by Your sharp sword
from the wicked who surround me. Give
them what they have deserved, O Lord.
Fill their bellies full of woe

and let their children also live
in grief and pain and fear, and so

on to their children's children, too!
Avenge me, Lord. Protect me. Do
this for Your faithful servant's sake,
and, from this nightmare, let me wake.

19

The sky proclaims God's glory and
the earth displays the work of His hand.
By day, we see the wonders here,
and nightly, orderly stars appear
to dazzle us. There is not a word,
but the message is clear to be seen and heard —
undeniable, intricate,
and grand, as we learn to admire it.
See how the sun emerges from
its bed in the east, like a bridegroom come
from the wedding chamber! Shield your eyes,
as it crosses the heavens in its precise
circuit. Its rays beam down and give
warmth and light to all who live.
The law of the Lord is perfect. The soul
rejoices in it and is made whole.
His testimony is sure and true,
and His precepts tell us what to do

and how to behave. What He commands
is wise, and the man who understands
and lives by His word is grateful for
instruction. Let us therefore adore,
indeed let us fear, the Lord, in awe
of His every ordinance and law.
Better than fine gold is His will.
Honey is sweet, but sweeter still
than the honeycomb's dripping is His thought
that teaches His servants what they ought
to do and aspire to. Who can
find fault in a reverent and docile man
who honors the Lord? He is kept from sin,
is tempted, perhaps, but does not give in.
Keep me blameless, O Lord. Let these
words of my mouth and of my heart please
You, who are my savior and my
rock — my hope for eternity.

22

My God, my God, how could You have
forsaken me? I cry by day
and night in pain to beg You: save
me! Yet You turn Your face away.

But still You are the holy God
Israel worships. In You our trust
is not misplaced. Our fathers had
deliverance. You were kind and just . . .

I am no more a man, but a worm,
despised and mocked. They jeer at me:
"If the Lord delight in such as he,
then let the Lord deliver him."

You took me from my mother's womb
and kept me safe upon her breast.

You are my God. I pray You, come
and help me. I am sorely pressed.

Great beasts surround me: monstrous bulls
of Bashan, snorting fire, paw
the earth, while the lion's ravenous jaw
gapes wide, and my bones' marrow chills

in terror. My limbs melt. My heart
runs like a ball of heated wax.
I tremble, weak in every part,
and endure the cowardly attacks

of friends and kinsmen who paw through
my household goods, as though I were
already dead.   I am helpless to
protest or drive away the cur

that scavenges and insults, unless
You come to my aid, and save me, bless
my soul, and drive it off. Restore
my strength, and I shall praise You for

Your miracles and justice. Men
will learn from me to fear Your name
when I shall stand in pride again
to testify how, in my shame

You did not hide Your face but heard
my prayer and to my desperate cry
gave ear. I shall broadcast Your word
and prove how You can satisfy

the starving and heal the sick, for You
are the hope of all the tribes and nations

who shall be grateful for how You do
justice on earth. The generations

shall celebrate Your goodness and praise
Your name as fathers and sons shall bend
their heads together in awe that stays
refreshed and that can never end.

23

Because the Lord is my shepherd, I
shall want for nothing. He leads me
by limpid waters and makes me lie
in rich and verdant pastures. He

restores my life. He guides me to
the paths of goodness, for His delight,
and even though I wander through
dark valleys, He keeps me in sight.

I fear no evil; He is near
protecting with His mighty staff
and comforting. What should I fear
from enemies? I sit and laugh

as I take my place at the table You
prepare. You anoint my head and fill
my cup to overflowing. Who
can doubt that goodness and mercy will

attend me during all the days
of my life? And I shall give thanks to
my Lord, and I shall sing His praise.

24

The earth is the Lord's, its yield and its
people. He has founded it on
the seas and rivers, so that it sits
solid and firm. And who shall ascend
the hill of God? He must be one
who is pure of heart and clean of hand
to stand on that holy place, whose soul
leaps only to the exaltation
of the Lord, and one who will not swear
falsely. On him, blessings fall
from the one God of his salvation,
that awesome spirit of Jacob's stair.

Selah

Lift up your lintels, O you gates,
and be lifted up you ancient doors.
Outside, the King of Glory waits.

Who is the King of Glory?
    The Lord in His force,
    the Lord of hosts.
He is the King of Glory.

Selah

25

A soul leaps up to greet You, Lord.
Be its protector; be my guide,
Constant when enemies press me hard,
Dangerous, scornful. Stay by my side

Every day, and teach me Your truth,
For Your narrow path is my only hope.
Give Your indulgence to faults of my youth.
Have pity whenever I stumble and grope

In blindness and clumsiness. Set me right.
Justice frightens me; mercy, grant.
Keep me always within Your sight
Like a child who wants to be good but can't.

My faults, pardon, and yet again.
No one adores You more than I,

O God. There are many more righteous men,
Praising Your name, but I try, I try.

Quarrelsome, frivolous, flighty, yes . . .
Redeem me, heal me, for Your own sake.
Sins are deplorable. Nevertheless,
Turn me around, correct my mistakes.

Under the glare of a cloudless sky,
Vileness is bleached by the sun all day,
White as the snow. So, You purify.
X-ray my cancerous lumps away.

You are my God. Oh, take me back.
Zeal may make up for those virtues I lack.

29

Acknowledge, admire, admit the Lord's
strength and a glory that's His alone,
      when the wind howls
      the endless vowels,
in His own voice, of His own words.

Recoil from the thunderclap: wince in the glance
of lightning that zigzags down from His throne;
      hear the gale's shriek
      and the cedars creak
as they break under His power and dance

as the mountains themselves seem to do — Oh, yes! —
naked, their cover of shrubbery gone.
      In awe, we stand by
      and in reverence cry,
"Glory to God! God bless . . . !"

34

Always, I shall bless my Lord,
Boast of His love, and demonstrate
Clearly to those who have not had
Deliverance from affliction the great

Easing He offers. Let us as one
Frame prayers of praise and thanks to Him.
God is more radiant than the sun.
His rays can penetrate to the dim

Interior places of the soul.
Just before we abandon hope,
Kind angels come, console, condole,
Lighting the dark through which we grope.

Magnificent! O taste and see!
Near at hand is abundant proof

Of the goodness of God. And happy are we
People who worship beneath His roof.

Quite awesome is He, and holy men
Revere and love Him, knowing He will
Save and protect them, confident when
They trust in Him, they may fear no ill.

Up on the veld, the lions' young
Voice in vain their hunger, but here
We are fed by the Lord. We wander among
Xeric wastes, and freshets appear.

Your faith may waver, but trust that His vast
Zig-zagging lines will converge at last.

39

I will behave myself and watch
my tongue, whenever I am in
the presence of some evil wretch,
lest it betray me into sin.

Let me not wish him ill, let me
keep quiet, even though I see
him thrive and prosper. Let me not
compare what he and I have got.
My heart's banked embers smoulder, then
will blaze up on occasion. When
this happens I turn to God to seek
His help. I feel abandoned, weak,
afraid. And then I pray: "Lord, you
have given me an inch or two,
but tell me how long is my span,
or rather how short. What is a man?
No more than a puff of wind? And is

the wealth and power he thinks is his
a shadow merely? Will a gust
of the breeze disperse it like all dust?
My hope — what hope I have, O Lord —
must be in You, and I turn toward
my God for protection. Idiots, knaves,
insult me. I am mute. God saves
me anyway, forgives my many
faults He has corrected, when He
acted as strict parents should
who'd make their children wise and good.
Jehovah, hear the fervent prayer
of a nomad in dry desert air.
Over the endless lifeless dunes
my voice resounds in plaintive tunes
my father's fathers sang. We're here
for only a moment. Lord, give ear.

41

Those who care for the poor are blessed,
and the Lord protects and loves them best,
guarding against their enemies' snares,
and when they are taken ill, He cares
for them and heals their infirmities.
I have tried to be one of these,
and I pray to the Lord, now that I lie
on a bed of pain and my enemies laugh
and complain how I take too long to die,
let Him be gracious on my behalf.
Let Him note who comes to visit
with hollow words of comfort — but then
outside, when companions ask him, "Is it
nearly time?" he nods. "And when
he's gone," he adds, "he will be forgotten,"
which prompts fresh gales of their mean laughter.
The friends I trusted most are rotten:

they've broken bread with me and after
that turned against me, and my heart
is broken. O Lord, I implore,
hear my prayer now. Take my part.
Defy them! Raise me up once more
as a mark of Your favor and my reward
for having at least tried to do
the righteous thing. Hear, my dear Lord,
an embittered soul that cries to You.

47

Clap your hands! Oh, shout and sing
in joy that the Lord, our God, the King
of all earth's peoples has decreed
the heritage of Jacob's seed.

                              Oh, sing!

Before the holy ark, then, shout
and let the choir of trumpets blare
God's praises. To our King, sing out
in counterpoint our fervent prayer:
God sits upon His heavenly throne,
and princes of all peoples bow
to acknowledge Abraham's God and how
the earth belongs to Him alone.

49

Nobles, commoners, rich and poor,
neighbors and strangers, lend an ear
to what I say. My mind is clear
and my mouth shall offer wisdom for
the common good. Take heart. Take note
of the song that issues from my throat.

The times are very bad, and yet
what should I fear from the evil men
around me everywhere who get
their hoard of wealth and trust it, when
no man can buy off God or fate?
What good are riches then? The great
must die as each of us will do,
the wise man and the stupid, too.
Spendthrifts perish, and those who save
will lie beside them in the grave.
The shows of the pompous do not last,

for bodies die and corruption fast
consumes us as if we were merely
beasts, a herd of sheep picked out
for butchering. We mill about
the pit that is Sheol: a fall
is waiting for us, one and all.
But God may yet redeem me from
that deep abyss and bring me home.

                                        Oh, sing!
Do not revere the rich, therefore,
who think themselves secure, but know
their wealth won't help them anymore
when they are dead. Naked, we go
out of the light, and wealth and fame
dissolve, and the wind will erase each name
inscribed on our memorial stones
above bare undistingushed bones.

51

Mercy, Lord, have mercy! Show
how great Your love can be. My sin
forgive, and again forgive, although
transgression is what I wallow in.
Against Your laws and You, I have
offended mightily. You are right
to turn away from me, but save
one who adores Your name, despite
my failings and corruption. I,
conceived in sin and thus brought forth,
dream nonetheless of purity.
Remind me of my spirit's worth.
Purge me with hyssop, and asperse
my soul to the whiteness of new snow
and hear as blessings every curse
I've uttered. Iniquitous, I know,
I'm not yet irredeemable. Make
me clean, revive my hopes, uphold

me for Your greater glory's sake.
My transformation may be told
among transgressors, who will turn
to You, as I did. I shall sing
Your praise. The flesh of sheep may burn,
but better by far is the offering
of a broken spirit, healed and restored
to what it always should have been,
obedient to Your holy word
contrite, and cleansed of every sin.

Likewise, repair Mount Zion, too;
rebuild once more Jerusalem.
What You have done for me, then do
for Abraham's children — all of them.

52

O mighty man, we hear you boast
of all the power you have to do
great harm to us. We hear how you
connive against us. You love most
what's evil and hate the good. You'd choose
lies every time over truth. Your tongue
is sharp as a razor and you would use
its wiles to cause great grief among
our people. But God will break you yet
and bring you down, or pluck you from
the land of the living, and we shall come
and laugh to see what He has set
for your punishment. You are unjust,
and foolish to have put your trust
in wealth and power and not the word
and love of the ever living Lord.

I am the olive tree that grows
and grows in God's courtyard and thrives
for generations and survives,
bearing its fruit as a way to show
gratitude to the Lord and proclaim
the strength and goodness of His name.

53

Whoever says in his heart *There is no*
God is a fool and an evil-doer.
From heaven, the Lord peers down below
to see if there be any who are

wise, or humble, seeking after
the God who made them. What does He find?
Depravity, impious laughter,
and cynicism among mankind.

Let those who do not fear the Lord
and prey upon His people quake
in fear that God will come down hard
upon them, scatter their bones, and make

the ungodly weep and Israel glad
that we have been delivered. Then
the Lord will restore what we once had
and Jacob shall rejoice again.

55

Hear my prayer, O God; do not
ignore me when I turn to you,
for I am sorely tried by what
my enemies say and what they do.
Spiteful, they harbor grudges, plot
against me, collude, and threaten to
destroy me. My heart is heavy. I
am filled with fear and trembling. Death
is everywhere. I want to fly
on the wings of the dove on the wind's breath
across the skies to the desert where
I'd hide myself. In safety there,
I'd sing my plaint. Destroy, O Lord,
my enemies. Confuse them, do in
their ramparts with Your avenging sword.
Wreak on their dwelling places ruin,
for they are liars, deceivers, frauds

who pretended once to be my friends
exchanging sweet and decent words.
But suddenly that pretence ends . . .
Let death take them, or better yet,
do not but let them go alive
to the gloomy depths of Sheol, and let
them languish there in fear and thrive
in the ghastliness of the grave. I call
upon my God to come and save me.
Morning, noon, and evening, all
I do is cry with the voice He gave me
that He may deliver me, for many
stand against me. Yet am I
protected by my Lord from any
villain who wishes me to die.
They shook my hand, and then they turned
traitors. Their speech was always smooth

as butter, but in their hearts there burned
the ugliness of war. The truth
comes out at last. I turn to the one
friend I can count on — God who keeps
watch on the good and evil done
before His eye that never sleeps.
Cast them into the deepest pit
that is blood and treachery's reward.
Kill them! Let me witness it,
and I will trust in You, O Lord!

56

All day long my foes oppress me.
Save me, gracious Lord, and bless me.
I am afraid and trust in You,
for, after all, what can flesh do

to me? They conspire together, plan
much mischief, stalk me . . . but You can
protect me, pay them back, in wrath
destroy those who impede my path

and wish me evil. You have kept
my troubles entered in your ledger.
The vial of tears that I have wept
is brimming full, and yet my treasure
is the Lord's word. And if this be
the case, what can they do to me?

I promise to give all honor to
my Lord for deliverance. Only You
can help me stand as I weave and fall:
You are my life, my light, my all.

58

Of what use are gods, if they do not
deal justly with men? But look at what
happens on earth, every day, to the good
who suffer as much as the wicked should.

Bad from the start when they lay in the womb,
they are naughty children and they become
evil men: as the poisonous snake,
is bad from the egg, so these are. Break

their teeth, O God, or rather say
their viper's fangs. Melt them away
like rivulets in sand. Beat down
their heads like grass that is trampled brown.

Let them dissolve like snails into
their own disgusting slime. Oh, do

justice and uphold the right.
As a pile of thorns can do, ignite

abruptly and, before our eyes,
destroy them, cleanse and cauterize.
Let us rejoice in their downfall, sweet
as any dream. Let us bathe our feet
in their iniquitous blood. No men
will doubt there's a God or justice, then.

59

O God, help me. I am beset
by enemies everywhere. They whet
long knives and cry out for my blood.
Deliver me from their evil, God.

Cut-throats and murderers combine
against me through no fault of mine.
I have been true to Your holy word.
Help the innocent, O Lord!

Every evening they assemble
to howl outside like dogs. I tremble,
at their protracted and bestial snarls.
I overhear their sordid quarrels

about who should strike first to tear
my tender flesh, but, Lord, You are there

to intercede in my behalf.
I trust in You, my God, and laugh

to think how You will kill them, or,
better, keep them alive before
your awesome power. Let them languish.
Together, we shall watch their anguish,

hear their curses, and delight
as they learn to recognize your might.
You are my protector! You
will do to them, and do, and do —
that men may know You. They will quake
in fear for Your name's awesome sake.

                       O Sing!

I hear them now as they mutter, prowl,
threaten, whimper, growl, and howl,

but I shall raise my voice as well
to praise the God of Israel

in whose great strength, I feel secure.
I am assailed, but I am sure
God will protect me. O God above,
keep me safe in Your steadfast love.

63

O God, you are my God! My whole
being longs for You. My soul
thirsts, and my flesh faints in yearning.
I am in a desert, dry and burning,
and in the distance, see a shimmer . . .
Mirage? Oasis? It is a glimmer
of what Your love is like. Sunstruck,
I stand erect to bless my luck.
In prayer I shall raise my outstretched hands
to praise Your name to the endless sands.

My soul reclines at a banquet table,
happy and sated, where I am able
to thank and bless You with my dry
and cracked lips. Or else I stretch out late,
as if in bed to meditate
how in the darkness You will keep
watch and protect me as I sleep.

My lids grow heavy and close, but I
continue, in dreams, to magnify
and sanctify my God. But those
who look to hurt me, or suppose
I am defenseless, let them be brought
abruptly low, as You know they ought.
Let them become the jackals' prey.
Stop up their lying mouths, I say
who shall testify to the endless glory
of God and recite His splendid story.

67

Bless us, God, give us Your grace,
and show to us Your shining face.
Your ways are right and sure and save
us all. Whatever here we have
we owe to You and thank You, O
great God in heaven. Men below
should sing and dance in gratitude.
You judge among us who is good
and who is not. You make the soil
in summer's heat and springtime's rain
reward us richly for our toil
which is, unless You bless it, vain.
From the ends of the earth, men look above
to You in thanks, and fear, and love.

69

Save me, God, from the turgid water
that up to my neck is already risen.
My feet in the bottom muck are caught, or
do I sink deeper into its prison?

My throat is dry, and my voice, gone.
Nobody heard me when I could shout;
now I must whisper, crying upon
my God whom I begin to doubt.

Enemies, Lord, are everywhere,
spreading about me vicious lies.
I've more of them than I have hair.
To You, O God, I lift my eyes.

You see into my heart; You know
my sins and failings, every one —

my guilt and its limits. You know also
how, for Your sake, I am undone.

I am a stranger to my own brother;
my parents have cast me out. I turn
to You, my immortal, heavenly father.
With longing for You does my soul burn.

Rescue me then, as a drowning man
who may be plucked, gasping, out of the waves.
Show those who mock what miracles can
accomplish — that You are the God who saves.

I have believed; I turn to You now,
desperate for pity if not relief.
I have been faithful. Do not allow
the faithless to laugh in their unbelief

at me and at You, but show us both
Your face that is awesome and awful, too,
when in Your ripeness You wax wroth.
Send down those pains so richly due . . .

Pour out Your anger, O God, pour down
that acid purification. Break
those to whom You are unknown.
Blot out their lives altogether. Make

of their dwelling places a desolation.
Afflict their wounded; wound their sick
in a dreadful and dazzling demonstration
of power as limitless as it is quick,

and I will sing canticles of praise
and thanks to my savior and creator

who both gives life and shows us the ways
of righteousness. (Which gift is greater?

Who can know?) Then, let us pray
that God may rebuild our crumbled walls,
that our children's children one day may
inherit and praise Him in these halls.

70

God, help me! Oh, God, hurry, come,
put them to shame, and strike them dumb
who plot against my life. Let them
who cry at me, "Aha, aha!"
suffer such pains as You condemn
them to in Your just anathema.

We love You and together voice
our prayers of praise. Let us rejoice.
But hear us, too, when we implore
Your help. On us who are weak and poor,
bestow Your majesty and might.
Deliver us, Lord, today. Tonight.

71

Protect me, Lord. Keep me from shame
and humiliation, now that I
am old. The wealth I had and the fame
are all gone, and in need, I cry

to You, my refuge. Be my rock
that You once were in my youth's prime.
Those rascals who threaten me and mock,
punish! I can recall a time

when people looked to me to show
how piety and devotion could
succeed. My foe is Yours also.
What good is there in being good

if lives like mine end badly? What
will mankind think? *He is easy prey.*

God may have done him favors, but
it could have been dumb luck, they'll say.

Use me to show Your strength. Defy
their insults, and with every breath
I draw, I'll praise Your justice, I
will thank You at the doors of death.

My eyes are dim; my hair is white.
Nevertheless, I'll sing before
my Lord to celebrate Your might.
Who is like You, O God? I implore,

raise me up in the eyes of men
who'll honor me if they honor You.
My harp will ring with music then
and my soul dance as it used to do.

My mouth will praise You and my face
glow as of old in Your love's light,
defying those who have brought disgrace
to a lover of piety and right.

77

My cries of pain disturb the gloom
of night: I stretch forth an upturned palm
to a pitying God who I assume
attends not only to prayer and psalm

but inarticulate whimper and groan
or to those with sufferings so acute
that they are altogether mute,
desperate, beleaguered, bereft, and alone.

Long ago, in happier days,
I lived in the Lord and with Him, but He
has averted His unblinking gaze
and forgotten what He promised me.

It cannot be, and yet it is
precisely so: His river of

compassion has run dry; in His
wrath He now withholds His love.

I will turn my thoughts to bygone days
to His holy works of word and deed,
and perseverate my songs of praise
for having, in our times of need,

redeemed the sons of Jacob. Wave
upon wave breaks on the shore. The wind
howls. The thunder crashes. Save
your people, God, though we have sinned.

Calm the gales and bid the sea
subside and part for us again.
Moses and Aaron's desperate men
and women You saved. O God, save me.

79

O God, the heathen have defiled
Your holy temple and all our city.
Barbarians have murdered mild
and saintly men and shown no pity

to women and children but have spilled
our blood like water on dry dirt.
Orphans and mothers of those who were killed
weep and comfort each other's hurt.

Pour out upon these gentiles, Lord,
Your wrath, because they have laid waste
Your people's lands. Their hearts are hard.
We plead with You to come in haste,

deliver us, forgive our sin,
and teach the pagans some respect

for You and justice. Come, begin
to let their fortresses be wrecked

and let us dance to hear them groan.
Visit on them, sevenfold, the same
hurts they did us, and then, as one,
we will give thanks to Your holy name
for ever and ever in hymns of praise
that our children shall sing to the end of days.

82

In the pantheon where they meet,
each god takes his proper seat.
> Their faces are masks
> as the Lord asks,
"How can you presume so long
to favor the wicked and wrong?"

> Selah.

"Rather it ought to be your
business to care for the poor.
> Keep the weak and needy
> from evil and greedy
men. Hear My words and obey.
You are leading the people astray."

Although they be gods in the sky,
nevertheless, shall they die
      as princes do
      and false gods, too.
For the Lord shall determine their worth
in heaven as here on the earth.

83

With my hand to my ear
I am straining to hear
        some whisper of Yours, my Lord,
but the tumult is loud
of Your foes — a great crowd,
        with evil intentions toward

Your people. They mean
to wipe the map clean
        of our country, erasing its name.
From Moab they come,
and from Gebel, and from
        Philistia bringing us shame.

They consort and conspire
with the people of Tyre,
        uniting to conquer the Jew.

The Assyrian horde
has joined with them, Lord.
    We pray You, now, O God, do

to them as You've done
at Jabin and Kishon,
        destroy them and turn them to dung
on the battleground there.
Let their nobles despair
        who threatened with insolent tongue

to take the Lord's fields
for themselves. Let their shields
        be whirled in the wind like the dust.
Like the wildfire, follow
through upland and hollow,
        pursue them, destroy them at last.

Disperse them, disgrace
those who laughed in Your face,
        dismay them and demonstrate, too,
with glory and might
and Your love of the right:
        the Lord in the Highest is You.

87

High on the holy mountain
the city of God gleams
more glorious than any
habitation of dreams.
Zion's gates stand open,
inviting. We aspire
to enter in from Babylon,
Philistia, and Tyre —
the places of our birth, and yet
we never felt at home
as we do now, when the Lord enrolls
His children who've come home
to dwell here in His city
where our hearts, at ease, may sing
His praise in a constant morning
of a never-ending spring.

88

O Lord, I call on You by day
and through the night. Hear what I say.
Let my groans and prayers arise
to You. Give ear to one who dies,
feeling his end upon him. It
is giddy here at the yawning pit.
My knees are weak; all strength is gone,
like corpses they heap dirt upon
and leave to moulder in their graves.
Your anger overwhelms me. Waves
break over me: I cannot draw
a breath. I founder, pitch, and yaw.
My friends desert me as I waste
away — they can't conceal distaste
and have exhausted pity. I
call out to You, my God. I cry
in fear and desperation. Do
the shades of the dead still pray to You?

Do breathless voices whisper out
of Sheol and Abaddon devout
blessings upon Your name? Do they
remember language and how to pray?
All night, like a small child, I've cried
to You in need, and yet You hide,
as if my helplessness and fear
were somehow pleasing to Your ear.
I lie in darkness and feel my life
ebbing away, as children, wife,
and friends near me dissolve — as I
shall do, when, presently, I die.

93

The Lord is clad in majesty.
Girded and robed in glory, He
is seated on a throne that never
moves and shall endure forever.

Stand on the shingle, watch the huge
waves that come crashing onto shore;
feel the power of each deluge
of water; hear it hiss and roar
in dismaying might . . . but mightier still
is God who made these deeps and will
note who has kept His laws and who
has worshipped as holy men should do.

97

The Lord in heaven reigns! Let earth
be glad, let great waves pound the beaches
in celebration. Clouds and darkness
surround Him and the truth He teaches.

A column of fire goes before Him
incinerating all His foes.
Bolts of lightning flash; we tremble
at the glimpses of truth that they disclose.

Towering mountains melt like wax
before His presence, and blue skies
proclaim His justice and His glory.
Idolaters must hide their eyes

as other gods bow down before Him.
But Zion watches and rejoices,

and Judah's daughters in a chorus
combine harmonious reverent voices.

You, O Lord, are the ruler of
the earth and heaven, land and sea.
Supreme, and just, You take delight in
those who hate iniquity

and You preserve Your holy scholars
and virtuous men and women. You
watch over them all night and keep them
safe to see the dawn renew

their fervent celebration. Hear them
thank You; note their songs of praise.
Rejoice in the Lord! Be glad, good people,
and do Him honor all your days.

100

Let every nation chorale to the Lord
a Dio, con brio
    in love and joy before Him.
    sing to Him, and adore Him

        with a resonant tonic chord,
        acknowledging God as the Lord.

He made us and all else there is.
We are His sheep; our meadow is His.
    In joy we intone our thanks and praise.
    Let us in elegant harmony raise
        our voices to sing:
            He is good, and He is one,
            from mother to daughter, from
                father to son.

102

Hear my prayer, O God, and let
my plaintive cry arise to You.
Give ear to me. I suffer, yet
I know that You can save me. Do!

My days are smoke that disappears
into thin air, while my bones burn.
My eyes are blinded by my tears.
I cannot eat or drink. I turn

to a pelican or vulture in
the wilderness, or, say, an owl.
All day, I listen to a din
of enemies' curses and taunts. I howl

like a crazed beast. Your disregard —
from anger or disgust? — is hard

to bear. Alone, in bed I lie
abandoned and I want to die.
As the slow, tormenting hours pass,
I wither like parched autumn grass.

But You, O Lord, on Your heavenly throne
will surely save, for pity's sake,
Zion for whom You have always shown
Your love. Make the nations quake

in fear and let their princes pay
homage to You when You appear
in righteousness, as the desperate pray
You will — and let the time be near.

The generations will record
Your miracles, telling their children how

the prisoners groaned until their Lord
set them free.   Oh, do so now,
that men in Zion may declare
the power of the Lord and prayer.

Here, at the race's mid-point I
feel myself falter. Lord, do not
take me before my time to die.
You will live forever, but what
You make on the earth will not last long.
A garment, it wears out, though You
will thrive and flourish, always young
refreshed and splendid, ever new,
and children of Your servants will
rejoice and praise Your glory still.

103

Praise the Lord, O my soul.
Let the soul of my soul praise
His name, exalt, laud, and extol
His kindness, remembering all the ways

He has forgiven our sins and healed
our sicknesses to save our lives.
Wherever we look, there is revealed
His generous bounty. His people thrives.

We are weak, we stagger and fall, but He
snatches us back from the pit. We rise
to a new day's bounty, surprised to be
sustained like the eagle that soars and flies
on powerful updrafts of air,
effortless, beautiful there.

He works, for those who are sorely oppressed,
deliverance, vindication. He made
His word understood by Moses and blessed
Israel's people — who disobeyed,

and yet He is merciful and forbears.
He is slow to anger and mollifies
His wrath. Because of His love, He spares
the sinner who repents and tries

and fails again and again atones.
Heaven is high above the earth,
and He is a father who loves His sons.
His pity is greater by far than our worth.
        Like the wildflower that grows,
        we wither away. He knows

how the wind will pass and the flowers be gone.
The love of the Lord nonetheless shall last
forever and righteousness be done
to our children's children. Over the vast

heavens, the Lord's high throne is set
and the angels bless Him and holy men
attend to His voice that is speaking yet,
and praise Him, and His ministers then
            will join in the praise and sing
            to the universal King.

109

O God, where are You? In this silence
all I hear is wicked lies,
a villain's insults, threats of violence . . .
I look up to empty skies

for help, and turn in need to You,
beset, despised for my good deeds.
An empty unremitting blue
glares down on me, and my heart bleeds.

Set some crook upon him, and let
that crook have lawyers. Let them sue.
Let his odd virtues count against him.
Number his days; let them be few.

Turn his children into orphans.
Let his wife be widowed. Make

his family mendicants. Let greedy
creditors their pittance take.

Let strangers ruin what he's planted.
Let no man pity his wife or child,
but let them suffer also. Let him
know this somehow. Drive him wild

with grief, remorse, chagrin, self loathing.
May his father's every sin
be in our minds forever. Let his
mother's name call forth a grin

from traveling salesmen. Oh, destroy them,
blot them utterly from the earth
for what he did and failed to do.
Let him regret from the day of his birth

every wicked thing he did
to the destitute. He loves to curse:
let him hear them in a torrent,
as bad as those he gave, and worse.

He clothed himself in curses: let him
wear that vile habiliment.
Let it soak his skin, suffuse his
joints and bones like liniment.

And may this be the fate of every
enemy who spreads such lies,
for I am indigent and weak,
with a stomach full of butterflies

and knees that have turned to water. I
cannot defy them, but Your name
is mighty. O my God, destroy them
and cover them, every one, with shame.

Their curses and insults are nothing
if you will bless me, Lord. My breath
shall praise your robust justice. Save me
from those who'd do me unto death.

113

Praise the Lord! Oh, praise
His name and His righteous ways.
Now and forevermore,
from first light to nightfall,
let us praise the Lord and adore
Him who is ruler of all.

To whom shall we liken our
God who presides in the sky,
raising the weak and the poor
to seat them in glory by
the sides of great princes and kings?
To the barren woman, He gives
children, a home — and she lives
in comfort the rest of her days.
For His works the universe sings
to the Lord, in prayers of praise.

114

When Israel from Egypt fled
the house of Jacob and crossed the Red
Sea, we found in Judah's hills
a home, a sanctuary. It fills
the heart to think. The ocean's wide
expanse ran out in a terrified
ebb tide, while the hills above them made
merry: the mountains, like lambs, played,
frisked, and gamboled, or so the peasants
say, who know and fear the presence
of Jacob's God and feel the awe
He should inspire. We who saw
that rock erupt with water pray
that He may protect us every day.

115

Not for our sakes, O Lord, but for
Your glory that men may adore
and bless Your name, we ask that You
may make us thrive and prosper to
silence each rude and scoffing nation.
Make a persuasive demonstration
of what You are. They worship mere
silver and gold figurines with eyes
that do not see, ears that can't hear,
objects than any person buys,
in a shop, like dolls to entertain
a child, and to these dolls they pray
for long life, health, fair weather, rain . . .
But Israel does not do as they.
The Lord is our help and shield, and we
trust in His strength and know that He
will keep the house of Israel and
of Aaron and will bless our land.

All those who fear Him, He will bless
and give increase. The heavens, yes,
are the Lord's, but He has given men
the earth. We must be grateful then
for all our lives, as long as we
have breath to worship Him: praise be
to God for life and light and for
the world, now and forevermore.

120

In anguish, I cry out to God
and pray that He may answer me,
"Deliver me, O Lord, from bad
faith, liars, frauds, mendacity."

What's recompense for a liar's tongue?
Sharp arrows or the glowing coals
of the broom tree! I sojourn among
men in Meshech who have no souls.
Too long I have dwelt in Kedar where
exotic flowers taint the air
and honesty and truth are rare.
(It's more than I know how to bear.)
The word for "peace" in their discourse
means only the pause between the wars.

121

I look up to the hills where the locals
worship their primitive gods, and I
defy them, supersitious yokels,
for my God made the earth and sky.

He does not ever drowse or doze
but watches over us to keep
us safe. We have nothing to fear from those
tribesmen up there, for while we sleep
the moon won't light their way.   Awake
under the sun's benevolent rays
the Lord will protect us and will take
good care of His people all their days.
Our comings and goings He will note
and to our lives His love devote.

124

If God had not . . .
      I say again:
If God had not
      been by our side
when the enemy fell upon us, then
they would have swallowed us alive
and burnt our corpses. We survive
      because He saved us.
      Say, "Amen."

The waters would have drowned our men
and women. We'd have been swept away.
Let us praise and bless God, then,
who preserved us for another day.
We would be struggling in the net
the fowler sets for little birds.

Now we are free, do not forget
the Lord's deliverance. Sing out words
of praise for God whose might and skill
made heaven and earth. He commands them still.

126

When Zion was restored,
it was as if the Lord
had ended a long, bad dream.
Now grown men and women seem
like children, who always laugh.
Those nations that used to scoff
now marvel at our changed fate
and say that the Lord has done great
things for us. And we
in gratitude agree.
Praise pours forth from the mouth,
as, down in the arid south,
the wadis freshen and run
with water that gleams in the sun.
May those who, in tears, must sow

reap in such joy and know
our cries of delight and our cheers.
We have dried our rivers of tears.
and, dazzled, we blink, having come
into peace and plenty — and home.

127

Unless the Lord erect the house,
the carpenters' work is in vain.
Unless the Lord watch over the city,
the sentinels, peering out on the plain
alert and diligent, do so in vain.
Rise up early and labor long,
till your muscles ache that once were strong.
       Unless the Lord
        give you reward
it is all pointless, all in vain.

Sons and daughters are gifts of God,
the arrows in a hero's quiver.
Bless them, but also bless the giver,
      for the Lord is great.
With sons shall you know no fear or shame
from enemies gathering near your gate.
      Love the Lord. Praise His name.

130

From profound depths I call, O Lord.
Hear me supplicating here.
Dear Lord, give ear.

Without your mercy, Lord, what man
could dare to come before You in
his state of sin?

My soul is waiting on the Lord;
I trust in His word as I wait
like a guard at the gate

who looks for the breaking of day. So I
stare at His sky all night
where His love's light

may pierce that dark through which Israel gropes,
as we pray for Him to redeem
us with its gleam.

131

O Lord, my heavy heart is not
lifted as it ought to be,
or have I squinted my eyes at what
is too remote and obscure for me
to understand? But let it go,
that effort to grow in wisdom. Let
me feel the calm that children know
when, on their mothers' breasts, they get
crooned to, held, and loved. Even so
teach me to love the Lord and trust
in Him as Israel always must.

133

How good it is, how sweet, when brother
sits down with his brother to break bread
and dwell in peace with one another.
The anointing oil upon the head
of priests can hardly occasion more
delight as it trickles down their faces
or the morning dew on Hermon, for
manifest in those times and places
is how the Lord's will can be fulfilled
and every troubled heart be stilled.

136

Give thanks to God, who is good,
                    for His love is eternal.
Give thanks to the God of gods:
                    His love is eternal.
Give thanks to the Lord of lords:
                    His love is eternal.

For His miracles and wonders:
                    His love is eternal.
For the intricate heavenly canopy:
                    His love is eternal.
For separating the earth and the sea:
                    His love is eternal.
For turning the darkness to light:
                    His love is eternal.
For the sun in the daytime:
                    His love is eternal.

For the moon at night:

> His love is eternal.

For doing Egyptian children harm:

> His love is eternal.

For setting of Israel's people free:

> His love is eternal.

For the strong hand and outstretched arm:

> His love is eternal.

For dividing the waves of the Red Sea:

> His love is eternal.

For letting us pass safely, then:

> His love is eternal.

For drowning all of the Pharaoh's men:

> His love is eternal.

For leading us through the trackless wastes:

> His love is eternal.

For smiting the Amorites, and Sihon:

> His love is eternal.

For Og of Bashan, whose people we slew:

His love is eternal.

For giving our people the lands of Zion

His love is eternal.

He remembers us in our tribulations:

His love is eternal.

He defends us from the hostile nations:

His love is eternal.

He feeds us as a parent does:

His love is eternal.

The God who is, will be, and was:

His love is eternal.

O give thanks to the God of heaven:

His love is eternal.

137

By the Tigris' banks we sat and cried,
and there by the Euphrates' side
        we wept, we wept,
        for in our hearts we kept
           Zion.
              We thought of Zion.

Our captors bade us sing, but we
hung on the weeping willow tree
        out under the stars
        our mute guitars,
           Zion.
              We thought of Zion.

How shall we sing in exile, how?
If I forget Jerusalem now,
        let my hand wither and my tongue,
        that in a thoughtless moment sung,

turn to a stone in my mouth.
I stare, in silence, south
    to Zion.
    We think of Zion.

Remember the Edomites. Think how they
destroyed Jerusalem that way!
How could we ever forget that day?
        You, Babylon,
        you babble on.
But your time will come, we say,
        who yearn for it and pray:
        An avenger will one day arise
        from earth or descend from empty skies
        to pluck out your little babies' eyes,
            and, as you stare in shock,
            crack their heads upon a rock.

139

O Lord, you have searched my soul and known
its innermost secrets. When I lie down
or rise up, even before I could start
to shape a thought, You see in my heart.
Whatever way I turn, I find
Your eye upon me, in front, behind.
Where, if I tried to, could I flee?
Above the earth? Beneath the sea?
In farthest lands where strangers dwell,
or no one at all? In the depths of hell?
Not even in darkness of night can I hide
myself from You who are by my side
and first put me together from
the dust, within my mother's womb.
I praise and fear You, because You know
where I've come from and where I go
and do not even need to look
as I follow the program in Your book.

How intricate Your thought, how grand!
It takes note of each grain of sand
and how the winds dispose them all.
Lord, You are vast, and I am small.
I pray You, then, protect me from
malicious and violent men who come
to break Your laws. With Your strong arm
defend me and do my enemies harm.
I hate them with a perfect hate
and trust in You who know my fate,
have seen into my soul and found
nothing offensive or unsound.
Preserve me so, O Lord, I pray,
and lead me in Your righteous way.

144

I bless the Lord who is my rock,
who hardens me and trains me for
the ordeal I must face, the shock
of combat in the coming war.
He is my protecting shield
and ally on the battlefield.

What is a man, O Lord, that You
look down on? He is like a breath;
his days are the fleeting shadows You
scarcely notice before his death.
Nevertheless, the heavens take
account of us, for Your name's sake.

You touch the mountain top with fire.
Lightning and thunder roll through the skies
for men to fear, if they cannot admire.
Save me from unbelievers' lies.

Help me, O God, and with Your hand
keep me from drowning. Bring me to land

and I will sing a new paean
in praise of You. My harp will ring
to celebrate Your triumphs. On
deliverance and reckoning
I shall endeavor to rhapsodize.
Those who do evil and utter lies

will gnash their teeth to hear me. You
will bless us with prosperity:
our sons will thrive and daughters, too;
our herds and flocks will multiply.
With glistening eyes, we shall turn towards
Your heaven, rejoicing to be the Lord's.

150

Hallelujah! Praise God, you
in His earthly temple. Angels, too,
in their heavenly congregation, praise
His might and the justice of His ways.
Praise Him for what he does and is.
Praise with the trumpets' fanfares His
magnificence. With harp and lyre
praise! In your song and dance, admire
and praise! With cymbal and snare drum,
with every twangle, flourish and thrum,
praise Him. And let each living thing
praise Him with every breath and sing:
        Hallelujah!